D1372258

Emotions & Eating

Understanding Obesity

Emotions & Eating

Joan Esherick

Mason Crest

Mason Crest
450 Parkway Drive, Suite D
Broomall, PA 19008
www.masoncrest.com

Printed in the United States of America.

Series ISBN: 978-1-4222-3056-5
ISBN: 978-1-4222-3059-6
ebook ISBN: 978-1-4222-8842-9

Cataloging-in-Publication Data on file with the Library of Congress.

Contents

KEY ICONS TO LOOK FOR:

 Text-Dependent Questions: These questions send the reader back to the text for more careful attention to the evidence presented there.

 Words to Understand: These words with their easy-to-understand definitions will increase the reader's understanding of the text, while building vocabulary skills.

 Series Glossary of Key Terms: This back-of-the book glossary contains terminology used throughout this series. Words found here increase the reader's ability to read and comprehend higher-level books and articles in this field.

 Research Projects: Readers are pointed toward areas of further inquiry connected to each chapter. Suggestions are provided for projects that encourage deeper research and analysis.

 Sidebars: This boxed material within the main text allows readers to build knowledge, gain insights, explore possibilities, and broaden their perspectives by weaving together additional information to provide realistic and holistic perspectives.

Introduction

We as a society often reserve our harshest criticism for those conditions we understand the least. Such is the case with obesity. Obesity is a chronic and often-fatal disease that accounts for 300,000 deaths each year. It is second only to smoking as a cause of premature death in the United States. People suffering from obesity need understanding, support, and medical assistance. Yet what they often receive is scorn.

Today, children are the fastest growing segment of the obese population in the United States. This constitutes a public health crisis of enormous proportions. Living with childhood obesity affects self-esteem, employment, and attainment of higher education. But childhood obesity is much more than a social stigma. It has serious health consequences.

Childhood obesity increases the risk for poor health in adulthood and premature death. Depression, diabetes, asthma, gallstones, orthopedic diseases, and other obesity-related conditions are all on the rise in children. Over the last 20 years, more children are being diagnosed with type 2 diabetes—a leading cause of preventable blindness, kidney failure, heart disease, stroke, and amputations. Obesity is undoubtedly the most pressing nutritional disorder among young people today.

This series is an excellent first step toward understanding the obesity crisis and profiling approaches for remedying it. If we are to reverse obesity's current trend, there must be family, community, and national objectives promoting healthy eating and exercise. As a nation, we must demand broad-based public-health initiatives to limit TV watching, curtail junk food advertising toward children, and promote physical activity. More than rhetoric, these need to be our rallying cry. Anything short of this will eventually fail, and within our lifetime obesity will become the leading cause of death in the United States if not in the world.

Victor F. Garcia, M.D.
Founder, Bariatric Surgery Center
Cincinnati Children's Hospital Medical Center
Professor of Pediatrics and Surgery
School of Medicine
University of Cincinnati

Words to Understand

metabolism: The chemical reactions in the body that provide the energy and nutrients necessary to sustain life.

cellulite: Fatty deposits beneath the skin that give a lumpy appearance.

diabetes: A medical disorder resulting in insufficient production of insulin.

hypertension: High blood pressure.

osteoarthritis: A form of arthritis caused by wear and tear on the joints.

sleep apnea: A sleep disorder where someone momentarily stops breathing.

Emotional Eating: Why "Just Say No" Doesn't Work

May 1, 2003

Dear Diary,

I can't believe I did it again. I promised I wouldn't. I told myself I could handle it. I said I'd get out of the house or go for a run or chew gum or do something else if I felt bad. This was supposed to be my chance to start over. You know, the first day toward a brand new me. So much for new beginnings.

I don't know what happened. The day started so well. I got up really early, went for a jog, showered, and even ate a good breakfast (just a cup of yogurt, some strawberries, and a muffin)—all before I had to leave for school at 7:15 A.M. I felt so energetic; I even stayed awake through Ancient History, my third-period class. By fifth period I started to feel hungry, but I skipped lunch and felt good about resisting today's pizza special. Everything was going great. I even began to hope that maybe I'd finally be able to beat this food thing once and for all. Maybe I didn't really have to be fat for the rest of my life. Maybe I could lose ten pounds by summer.

Then that Tony Penella had to go and say something: "Hey Blubber Butt! Got some Jell-O to go with that jiggle?" Right in front of the whole seventh-period class!

My face flushed, and I felt like dying of embarrassment, but I did my best to ignore him. That was my one small victory today. I ignored Tony and didn't cry. I really wanted to scream or punch him or something. But I didn't.

I was so angry, though. As soon as I got home I ate everything I could get my hands on: a whole package of chocolate chip cookies; a pint of tin roof sundae; two English muffins; celery and peanut butter; half of a bag of pretzels. I couldn't stop myself. I just stuffed and stuffed and stuffed myself until I felt so full I thought I'd explode. At least there wasn't any candy in the house; I would've eaten that, too.

But I felt better; I wasn't so mad anymore. Eating's funny that way; it's weird how it makes me feel better for a while. The good feelings don't last though; I just start to feel lousy about myself again. And fat. Always fat. How can food be my worst enemy and my best friend?

What's wrong with me, Diary? Why can't I quit eating like this? I was okay until Tony opened his big mouth. Why do I eat when I'm mad or sad? Why do I feel so guilty? Why am I so stupid, so disgusting, and so completely unable to control myself? Why am I so fat? Will I always be this way?

Yours forever,
Morgan

Morgan is a fourteen-year-old high school freshman. Thick, wavy, shoulder-length hair frames her clear complexion and pretty smile. Her hazel-green

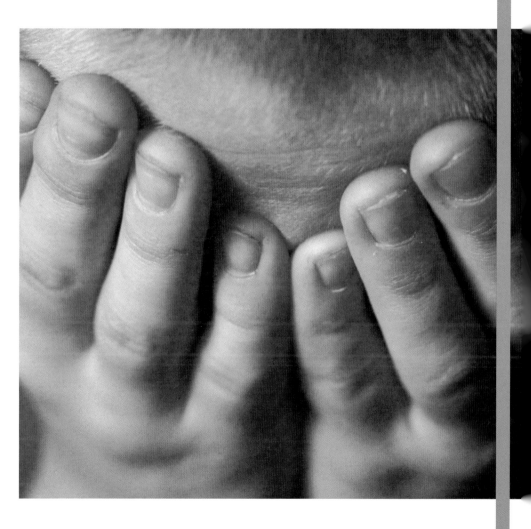

eyes sparkle with intelligence, humor, and authenticity. With broad shoulders and a muscular build, Morgan looks like an athlete—the kind you might see playing softball or throwing discus at a track meet. She's not rail thin like a marathoner, nor is she the image of size-one starvation chic like so many of her friends. But she's not grossly overweight either. She's a solid, well-proportioned teenager who happens to have a larger frame than her petite peers. Yet, when she looks at herself all she sees is fat: offensive, obscene, disgusting fat.

She's tried every diet she's heard of: liquid-only plans; food fasts; high-protein diets; low-carb diets; reduced-calorie diets; certain food combinations that supposedly increase **metabolism** and cause better calorie burn; she's even tried some of the menu plans touted by her favorite celebrities. The result is always the same: quick loss of a few pounds until something makes her angry or sad or jealous or stressed. Then she goes off the plan, starts eating like she used to, and the weight comes back again. After gaining a few pounds, she feels worse about herself than she did when she started dieting: *What's wrong with me? I hate my body. Why can't I control myself? See, I'm always going to be fat! I don't deserve to be thin. I'm such a screw-up! It's hopeless*—these thoughts plague her, and then, in her distress, she eats some more.

Diets won't work for this frustrated teen. They probably never will. Why? Because, like many of us, Morgan is an emotional eater. And food is everywhere.

Food, Food Everywhere

Think about your food intake. How much of what you eat do you consume strictly for nutritional benefit? How often do you grab a certain snack because you want to replenish the nutrients and vitamins your body has used? If you're like most people, it's not very often. You may not consider nutritional value at all. You'd rather load your lunch tray or dinner plate with foods that tempt your taste buds or make you feel good.

Think about when you eat. Do you eat only when you're hungry and stop when you're full? Many people don't. Why? Because physical need isn't the only reason we eat, especially in North America. Look back over the past seven days. Did you graze on junk food because you were bored or lonely? Did you "clean your plate" because you didn't want to waste food or offend someone? Did frustration lead you to gorge on cookies or candy bars? Maybe stress drove you to devour more food than you really wanted. Again, if you're like the average person, you've probably experienced these eating patterns at least once in the past week.

Make Connections: Common Foods Associated with Events or Activities

Try the following quiz. Name the foods that are most commonly associated with these activities or holidays:

1. Birthday parties
2. Going to the movies
3. Halloween
4. Thanksgiving
5. Valentine's Day
6. Boxing Day (Canada)
7. Sporting events (baseball games, hockey games, etc.)
8. Classroom parties in schools
9. Early-morning meetings or practices
10. Camping/hayrides/bonfires
11. Fairs or carnivals
12. Dances or proms

Answers: (1) cake and ice cream; (2) popcorn and soda pop; (3) candy; (4) turkey, stuffing, potatoes, and pumpkin pie; (5) chocolate; (6) fruit, nuts, boxes of food for the less fortunate; (7) hot dogs, Cracker Jack, peanuts, etc.; (8) home-baked cookies, cupcakes, candy, pretzels, chips, pizza, ice cream; (9) doughnuts, danish, bagels, fruit, coffee; (10) hot dogs, roasted marshmallows, s'mores (graham cracker, chocolate, and roasted marshmallow), hot cider, hot chocolate; (11) potato pancakes, cotton candy, caramel apples, popcorn; (12) punch, hors d'oeuvres, pre-dance dinners out

Think about customs related to food: holidays, family gatherings, social events, potluck dinners, prom dates, pizza parties, birthdays, graduations, weddings, and religious observances. Do you ever eat at family celebrations? Do you help yourself to donuts or coffee cakes at early-morning practices or meetings? Do you ever eat cake or ice cream on your birthday? Do you go out for pizza with friends? You probably do.

We eat for many reasons! North Americans and people around the world celebrate with food. We mourn with food. We study with food. We converse over food. We view movies with food. We shop with food. We exercise with food. We party with food. We drive with food, play games with food, and watch sporting events with food. Food, simply put, is part of our way of life; we cannot separate food from our culture.

We eat because we're hungry, because we need to, because we enjoy certain flavors, because it's part of our customs or family traditions, and we eat because we want to. Sometimes we eat just because the food is there. So what's a person like Morgan to do? Dieting or avoiding food will only set her up for failure in her weight-loss attempts or cause feelings of deprivation when everyone around her is eating. She can't make food disappear from her surroundings the way a recovering alcoholic throws out the beer he has hidden in his refrigerator. The weight-conscious teen can't promise to never eat again or avoid every event where food is served. Morgan will never succeed in overcoming her eating issues if she assumes food is her problem.

Food itself can't be the issue; plenty of people eat regular meals and participate in cultural eating fests without becoming overweight or needing to diet. Food is part of our lives and well-being. Our bodies require nourishment to stay healthy. We need food to stay alive. No, food itself doesn't create our problem; it's how we *use* food.

Feeding Our Emotions

High school seniors Samantha and Erin are bored and restless. They drive to the twenty-four-hour diner for club sandwiches, fries, and milkshakes.

Sixteen-year-old Jake feels overwhelmed by studying for his college placement exams. Instead of hitting the books, he heads to the local ice cream shop.

Thirteen-year-old Sadie's parents are bickering about her again. She grabs her jean jacket, storms out the door, and walks to the corner drugstore for whatever chocolate she can find.

Like these teenagers, we often turn to food for comfort, entertainment, stress-relief, escape, or emotional outlet. We use food to handle our feelings. We confuse emotional hunger with physical hunger. We think that satisfying the rumblings in our stomachs will satisfy the cravings in our souls. When we use food this way—eating to ease our feelings—we become emotional eaters. Most of us have been emotional eaters at one time or another.

Edward Abramson's book, *Emotional Eating: What You Need to Know Before Starting Another Diet,* cites a review of seven different studies on emotions and eating. Seventy-five percent of people in these studies reported that they ate in response to anger, depression, boredom, anxiety, and loneliness. Three out of four people admitted to emotional eating habits. In a classroom of twenty-eight teenagers, that would be twenty-one emotional eaters.

The statistic is even higher for those who struggle with being overweight. Abramson cites one study in which 84 to 100 percent of obese women fall prey to emotional eating.

So what's the big deal? What difference does it make if we're emotional eaters? You might argue that emotional eating is a perfectly safe way to handle negative emotions. You might say that handling emotions with food is at least better than turning to drugs or promiscuous sex or other self-destructive behaviors. You might think that emotional eating is nothing to worry about.

You'd be wrong.

The Risks of Emotional Eating

Left unchecked, emotional eating can be dangerous, even deadly. When we turn to food to handle our feelings we can become overweight or obese. An overweight person is someone whose body weight exceeds that recommended in established medical standards for a person of his or her height. An obese person is someone whose percentage of body fat is higher than recommended guidelines. Not all people who are overweight are obese. A bodybuilder or trained athlete, for example, has

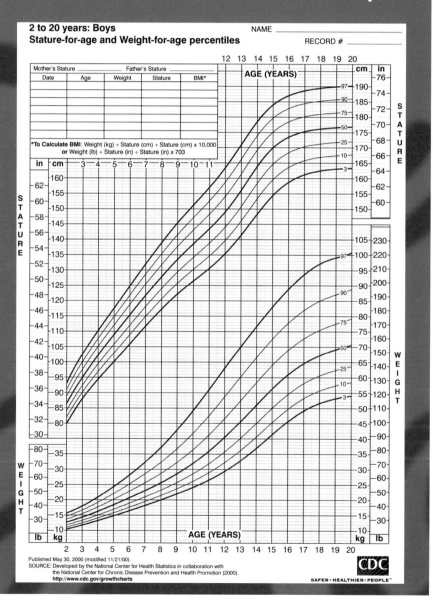

2 to 20 years: Boys
Stature-for-age and Weight-for-age percentiles

NAME _____

RECORD # _____

Mother's Stature _____ Father's Stature _____

Date	Age	Weight	Stature	BMI*

*To Calculate BMI: Weight (kg) ÷ Stature (cm) ÷ Stature (cm) x 10,000
or Weight (lb) ÷ Stature (in) ÷ Stature (in) x 703

AGE (YEARS)

STATURE

WEIGHT

Published May 30, 2000 (modified 11/21/00).
SOURCE: Developed by the National Center for Health Statistics in collaboration with
the National Center for Chronic Disease Prevention and Health Promotion (2000).
http://www.cdc.gov/growthcharts

CDC
SAFER · HEALTHIER · PEOPLE™

Make Connections: Centers for Disease Control and Prevention's Pediatric Growth Chart for Girls

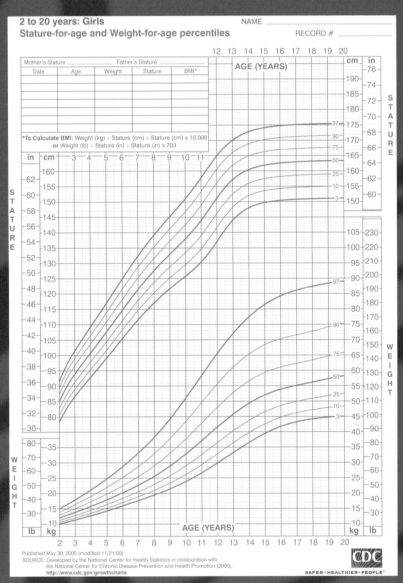

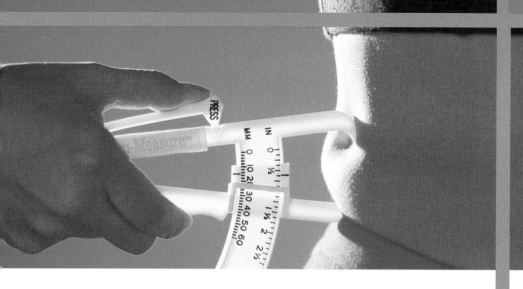

more muscle mass and weighs more than the average person of his height, but his percentage of body fat is lower. He may be overweight, but he is not obese. That's why it's important to consider both weight compared to height *and* percentage of body fat to determine overall fitness.

You might wonder if you're in danger of becoming overweight or obese. How can you tell? One of today's most commonly used measures is your body mass index (BMI). The higher your BMI, the greater your weight compared to your height and the more likely you are to be overweight or obese. BMI, however, does not measure how much fat your body carries, so BMI alone can't determine your fitness level. Two teenagers can be exactly the same weight and the same height (resulting in the same BMI), but one might be physically fit with well-defined muscles and little fat, while the other might be round, out of shape, and loaded with **cellulite**.

According to the National Institute of Diabetes and Digestive and Kidney Diseases, a branch of the U.S. National Institutes of Health, being over-weight or obese puts you at risk for **diabetes**, heart disease, stroke, **hypertension**, gallbladder disease, **osteoarthritis**, **sleep apnea**, breathing problems, and some forms of cancer. It also puts you at greater risk for psychological disorders, including depression. That's why emotional eating can be so dangerous. Not only does it prevent you from handling emotions appropriately, it jeopardizes your physical health and mental well-being.

Make Connections: Calculate Your BMI

BMI stands for body mass index. Your BMI is a number that reflects the relationship of your height to your weight. It is calculated using a simple math formula. People with high BMIs tend to be at risk for many diseases. People with mid-range BMIs tend to be healthier and more fit. People with low BMIs are generally underweight. Use the following formulas to determine BMI for people who are over twenty years old.

[weight in pounds ÷ (height in inches squared)] x 703 = BMI
OR
weight in kilograms ÷ (height in meters squared) = BMI

According to the U.S. Centers for Disease Control and Prevention, if your BMI is:
below 18.5, you are underweight
between 18.5 and 24.9, you are normal weight
between 25.0 and 29.9, you are overweight
at 30.0 or higher, you are obese

Emotional eating can also lead to eating disorders: anorexia nervosa (fear of eating, refusal to eat) and bulimia nervosa (alternating between extreme binging and purging patterns) are more prevalent among teenagers today than at any other time in history. According to the National Association of

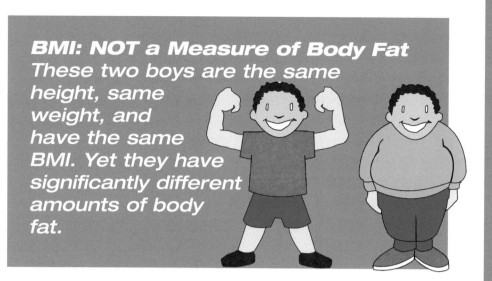

BMI: NOT a Measure of Body Fat
These two boys are the same height, same weight, and have the same BMI. Yet they have significantly different amounts of body fat.

Anorexia Nervosa and Associated Eating Disorders (ANAD), over seven million American women and one million American men have eating disorders. Eighty-six percent of these developed their disorders before they reached twenty years of age, 10 percent before age ten, 33 percent between ages eleven and fifteen, 43 percent between ages sixteen and twenty. For many, emotional eating was the first step to developing a lifelong full-blown eating disorder.

Emotional eating puts us at medical risk: risk of weight gain, risk of becoming obese, risk of developing eating disorders, risk of psychological problems, risk of future disease. It would make sense, then, that we just refuse to eat when we're stressed or feeling bad. It's not that easy, though.

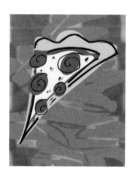

"Just Say No" Won't Work

Fourteen-year-old Morgan, if you remember, wasn't obese (she was just overweight), and she didn't have a true eating disorder, but she obsessed about her size. She wanted to be thinner and more petite, like

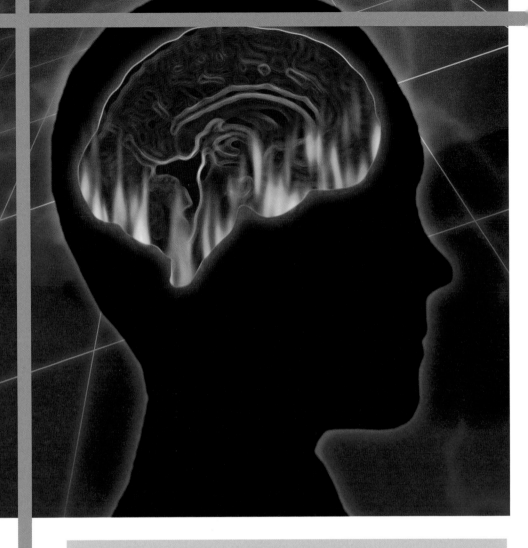

Research Project

This chapter mentions eating disorders: anorexia and bulimia. Use the Internet to do some research. Find out how emotional eating might be connected to these eating disorders. Why do experts think these disorders are so common today?

her friends, so she tried dieting and exercise. On the first day of her latest weight-loss attempt (recorded in her diary at the start of this chapter), she did wonderfully until a bully teased her. His words cut deep; she felt hurt, embarrassed, and angry, but she said nothing. Instead of showing any emotion or confronting her peer, she later gorged on snacks to ease her heartache and escape her pain. Her emotional eating sabotaged her dieting and fitness efforts. Like 75 percent of the population, she used food to handle her feelings.

This is exactly why diets, and the "just say no" approach won't work for Morgan or those of us like her. Diets, starvation, weight-loss plans, and pills don't address the underlying reasons we eat. Until we understand the relationship between emotions and eating, and then learn alternative ways of handling our feelings, we'll likely revert to emotional eating habits when we're stressed or feeling sad.

The next several chapters will look at our emotions, why we eat the way we do, and how to overcome emotional eating. They will also track Morgan's progress as she, too, learns about emotional eating and how to better handle her feelings.

Words to Understand

nutrients: Substances that provide nourishment.
ironically: Occurring in a manner opposite of what
would be expected.

Chapter 2

Defining Your Feelings: Emotions That Lead Us to Overeat

- Common Emotions That Result in Overeating
- Basic Ways Emotions Cause Us to Eat
- Emotional Eating Patterns

July 10, 2003
Dear Diary,

Mom took me to a doctor today. Not like my regular doctor—a counselor. This lady is supposed to know a lot about eating disorders and food addictions. I never would've gone, but Mom caught me raiding the fridge at two o'clock in the morning the other day. I was so embarrassed and ashamed when she found me eating alone in the middle of the night. I almost threw up. Mom just stood there looking at the empty ice cream containers, candy wrappers, and chip bags on the counter. She didn't say a word. She just looked at me for a long time, then turned around and went back upstairs. She didn't know I was upset about what happened at the community pool earlier that day, and I couldn't explain it. All I knew was that Jenny's comment about my bathing suit looking too small on me (or my thighs being too big) made me really self-conscious. I was hurt, too, and maybe angry. I don't know. But I couldn't sleep; I kept thinking about what Jenny said and how much it hurt me, and the next thing I knew I was in the kitchen devouring everything in sight.

The next day, Mom asked me to explain. But I couldn't; I didn't really understand it myself. That's when she said we should talk to someone who knew about eating problems.

Anyway, this lady seems okay. I'm supposed to call her "Dr. B." Her last name is some long Russian or Polish name—I can't even pronounce it. "Dr. B." is fine with me. We spent a long time talking. Well, it was more like her asking a lot of questions and me answering. I'm embarrassed to talk about some things, though. I think she kind of guessed that. So she gave me an assignment. I'm supposed to keep a "food and emotions journal." In it I'm supposed to write down everything I eat, when I eat it, and what I was feeling before I ate, while I was eating, and after I was done. She even gave me a list of words that describe emotions to choose from. Sometimes I don't know what I feel, so the list will help. I only have to do this for two weeks for now. I think she's just trying to get me to express (honestly) how I feel. We'll see how it goes. I'll let you know.

Yours forever,
Morgan

Morgan's mother took her to see a counselor because Morgan's emotional eating was spinning out of control. When she felt stressed or hurt, she binged until she felt sick, then she condemned herself for being such a "pig." Morgan felt trapped, but she didn't know how to express what was happening to her. Her counselor knew how to help. Morgan's recovery from emotional eating had to begin with Morgan learning to identify her feelings. If Morgan knew what she felt, she could learn ways of dealing with her emotions in healthier, more appropriate ways.

The same is true for us. Learning to identify our feelings is the first step to overcoming emotional eating patterns.

Common Emotions That Result in Overeating

Identifying emotions can be more difficult than it first appears. We don't usually experience just one emotion at a time. Imagine bumping into your steady boyfriend or girlfriend while he or she is out on a date with someone else. Would you be angry? Of course! Would you feel hurt? Certainly. Would you feel betrayed and jealous? You bet. All these feelings would swirl through your heart and mind as you wrestled with what your accidental encounter means. You wouldn't just feel one emotion.

Let's imagine that your parents just announced they are getting a divorce. What would you feel? Sad? Angry? Guilty? Helpless? Confused? Scared? Hurt? Probably all of the above. No single emotion could describe how devastated you might feel.

What about a positive event? Imagine passing your driver's test and earning your first driver's license. You'd undoubtedly feel proud, excited, happy, and maybe even a little nervous at the prospect of driving alone for the first time.

**Make Connections:
Are You an Emotional Eater?**

Identify the following statements as either true or false:

1. I eat when I'm bored to help pass the time.
2. After an argument with my parents or a friend, I sometimes eat to calm myself down.
3. When I'm sad, eating makes me feel better.
4. I snack when I'm studying for an exam or working on a project.
5. I eat more often when I feel stressed.
6. When I feel bad about myself, I punish myself by eating more.
7. When I'm happy or achieve something, I eat to celebrate.
8. When life feels out of control, eating helps me feel more in control.
9. When I fail at something, I eat to comfort myself.
10. If someone puts me down, I don't usually reply, but will eat more later.

If you answered "true" to five or more of these statements, you are probably an emotional eater. The more "true" responses you have, the greater your difficulty with emotional eating.

Emotions don't come to us one at a time and in isolation. Most emotions are intertwined with others. Weight-loss experts and emotional-eating researchers have pinpointed specific emotions that tend to trigger emotional eating more than others. The following list of eating-inducing emotions assumes that the emotions listed are only part of several we experience at any given time. Identifying these, even when they are mingled together, can help us see how they might fuel emotional eating.

- *Boredom*: that feeling of restlessness or fatigue we get when nothing stimulates us or holds our interest.
- *Loneliness*: when we feel cut off from other people and miss their company, we experience loneliness. We can be sad because we feel left out, isolated, or alone, or we can just long for greater interaction with people, but in both cases, we're lonely.
- *Anxiety/stress*: whenever we feel uneasy or overwhelmed about an impending event or situation (anything from an approaching thunderstorm to too much homework to a night out with a boyfriend to tomorrow's exam). Have you ever anticipated how difficult an upcoming exam might be? Have you ever felt nervous about what your future might hold? Have you ever felt like you had too much to do and not enough time to do it? These are forms of anxiety.
- *Fear*: similar to anxiety, it's just more extreme. Fear happens when we're filled with concern. We expect the worst. We anticipate something terrible happening. Anxiety can result from negative or positive things (we might be anxious about going on a date, for example). Fear, on the other hand, involves something negative and unwanted.
- *Helplessness*: when things happen that we can't control, a common emotional response is to feel like we can't do anything to change the situation. This feeling of inability to do anything is helplessness. For example, what do car accidents, deadly diseases, and natural disasters (tornadoes, earthquakes, and so on) have in common? They are

all things we can't prevent or control. We also can't control whether or not someone likes us, approves of us, or includes us in their lives.

- *Sadness*: that feeling of unhappiness that comes when we experience disappointment or loss. Everyone has a "down" day now and then. We all experience "the blues." We've all had our feelings hurt and experienced heartache; it's just part of being human. Maybe we didn't get the presents we wanted for Christmas or Hanukkah or Kwanzaa. Maybe our best friends moved away. Maybe our Golden Retriever got run over in traffic. These losses hurt us; they make us sad. But we grieve these things and move beyond them. If we don't, we may end up depressed.

- *Bitterness/resentment*: (when we don't get the treatment, recognition, or praise we think we deserve). Let's face it. Life just isn't fair sometimes. Someone else gets the credit for the project we worked hard on. We get blamed for something we didn't do. We do the right thing and nothing happens; someone else cheats and gets ahead. When these things happen, we can feel the need to get even or we can want to punish the people we resent. But we rarely act on these feelings. Instead we keep them bottled up inside. When we do, they can result not just in emotional eating but in depression as well.

- *Depression*: an emotion that's far more involved and complicated than sadness or bitterness. It affects not only our emotions but our bodies, too. Depression can actually cause (and result from) changes in the amounts of certain chemicals in the brain. When a person is depressed, she can't just "snap out of it." She may have trouble concentrating, sleeping, and remembering things. She may also feel fatigued, hopeless, and cry easily about seemingly little things. She may lose interest in favorite activities or hobbies, may worry a lot, feel worthless, and think or talk about death. Depression is a serious disorder that needs to be handled by a qualified health care provider. If you suspect that you or a loved one may be depressed, get help from a trusted medical professional as soon as possible.
- *Frustration*: a mix of discouragement and anger we feel when something prevents one of our goals, hopes, dreams, or expectations from happening. Something we wanted to occur didn't; someone prevented it from happening; some failure on our part kept it from working out as we planned. The blocked fulfillment of our desire results in frustration. The key to identifying frustration is its association with a disrupted goal, unsatisfied desire, or unfulfilled dream.

These emotions—when not handled in healthy, appropriate ways—often result in emotional eating. Have you experienced them? Do you ever eat when you feel these ways? The first step to overcoming emotional eating is recognizing these emotions when we experience them.

Basic Ways Emotions Cause Us to Eat

The next step is to understand why emotions drive us to eat. In the next two chapters we'll look at how the biology and chemistry of our bodies affect the way we eat, but for now we'll identify some basic connections between these emotions and our eating responses. The connections are pretty obvious; they are rooted in common sense.

Take boredom, for example. We eat when we're bored because we're looking for something to do. It's that simple. Consuming food is easy to do, convenient, and pleasurable. Bored? Why not eat? It feels good and will help pass the time. At least that's what we tell ourselves.

Loneliness is a little more complicated. We eat when we're lonely for many reasons: we may want to "treat" ourselves (since no one else will) and make ourselves feel special; we may want to fill up the emptiness we feel inside with something (anything) so we can feel better. We may want to distract ourselves from the pain of being alone. Food gives us something to think about other than how badly we feel.

Anxiety and stress can drive us to eat for different reasons. When under stress, we sometimes justify our eating by telling ourselves we need more **nutrients** to get through whatever it is we're worried about. Or we eat to calm ourselves down. Chemicals in certain foods can have a biologically calming effect (see later chapters for more detail), so we might turn to food for these chemically induced effects. Or we simply might use food for distraction.

Fear can make us not want to eat at all or it can do the exact opposite. Scientists have documented that fear, like other emotions, produces physical changes in our bodies: our pupils get bigger, our hearts beat faster, we perspire more, more blood flows to our brains and muscles, less blood flows to

our stomachs and intestines. Our bodies automatically do these things in response to fear to protect themselves from harm if attacked. These changes can make us feel hungry when otherwise we would not be. They can also make us lose our appetite for a period of time, after which we will become hungry again. In both cases, we may eat to satisfy our physical cravings.

Helplessness, unlike fear, has more to do with emotional responses than physical ones. When life feels out of control—when we feel helpless—we sometimes eat just to prove we can control something. Eating is something we can do, even when we feel like there's nothing we can do anywhere else.

Bitterness and resentment, like helplessness, lead us to eat just so we can take at least some kind of action. Sometimes we think, *I'll show you*, and then storm off to eat three orders of french fries at a local fast-food place. **Ironically**, our desire to punish the people we feel have treated us unjustly (or have been wrongly rewarded) results in our only punishing ourselves.

Sadness and depression drive us to eat in several ways. Some are rooted in our body chemistries (cravings brought on by chemical changes depression can bring); and some are emotional in nature (the desire to punish, reward, or comfort ourselves). At the very least, eating is pleasurable, and when we're sad or depressed we want to feel better. Eating feels good for a moment, so we eat to experience pleasure during a time that otherwise feels bad. We'll look at other links between sadness/depression and emotional eating in more detail in chapter 4.

Frustration is often the flip side of helplessness. They go hand-in-hand. We eat when we're frustrated because eating is again something we are able to do, even when our hopes or expectations don't come to pass. We eat to rebel, to show "them" (the people who blocked our dreams) they are wrong. If the source of our frustration is our own failure, then we may eat to punish ourselves, thinking things like *I'm such a screw-up; I deserve to be fat.* Eating when we're frustrated may satisfy us for a short time, but it will only lead to greater frustration later on.

We feel these things and then eat in response. As we'll learn later, however, emotional eating only hurts us in the long run. It won't solve our problems. Understanding our emotions and how they impact our eating habits can help us avoid further harm. Once we've identified specific emotions and understand how these emotions create a desire in us to eat, we can then look for patterns in the way we eat.

Emotional Eating Patterns

Tyrone, Hailey, and Sonya sit next to each other in math class. All three attend classes regularly, practice good study habits, turn in their assignments on time, and make good grades. The three eighth-graders have similar abilities: each tested well enough to be placed in an advanced class. They also have similar levels of self-confidence. All three are emotional eaters—but they handle the stress of their upcoming mid-term exam in different ways.

Tyrone nibbles. He keeps a bag of pretzels on his desk in his bedroom so he can munch while he's working on review problems. When he feels stressed or stuck on a problem, he grabs a handful of pretzels and crunches away. After an hour of studying, he realizes he's eaten an entire 14-ounce (396.9 g) bag—and it's the second bag he's gone through in one day.

Hailey, on the other hand, grazes. Feeling overwhelmed by some of her math problems, she gets up from her desk and heads to the kitchen. After rummaging through the pantry, she tries eating a few graham crackers, but they don't satisfy her cravings. She heads to the fridge. A piece of leftover pizza she finds there still doesn't do the trick, so she moves to the freezer. One ice cream sandwich and two popsicles later, she still hasn't had enough. Maybe the bag of M&Ms in her father's desk drawer will satisfy her. Grabbing the bag from his rolltop in the study, she heads back to her bedroom. An hour later, after polishing off the candy, she's cruising the kitchen again.

Meanwhile, Sonya diligently plows through her math review. She works hard for a solid four hours. By the time she's done, she's ravenously hungry. It's almost midnight when she begins her eating frenzy in the kitchen. Everyone else in the family is asleep; she has the kitchen to herself. Before she knows it, she's consumed an entire container of ice cream, two dozen cookies, a "family size" bag of tortilla chips, and a box of donuts. She washes it all down with a two-liter bottle of soda. Sonya binges in secret to relieve her stress.

Your way of eating in response to emotions may differ from mine. You may nibble like Tyrone, graze like Hailey, or binge like Sonya. All three responses are emotional eating habits. We differ from one another. We have

Make Connections: Types of Emotional Eating

Authors and researchers call different emotional eating styles by various names, but virtually all agree that these are the most common emotional eating patterns:

- *grazing*: eating whatever is available, moving from one food to the next with no plan in mind
- *nibbling*: getting more than half of your daily calories from snacks, not meals
- *sneaking*: eating on the sly, hiding your eating habits from others
- *binging*: gorging yourself to the extreme over short amounts of time
- *feasting*: eating oversized portions of food (healthy or unhealthy) at meals

Research Project

Keep track of your emotions over the course of a week by jotting down in a journal one word that describes your feelings several times throughout the day. In the same journal, keep track of everything you eat. Don't try to control what you eat for this project; just eat whatever you normally would. At the end of the week, look back at your journal. Do you seen any patterns between your emotions and what you eat? How about your emotions and when you eat? If so, which emotions were most connected to eating for you?

different personalities, different means of coping with stress, different emotional makeups, different backgrounds, different problems, and different aptitudes for exercise. What works for one person may not work for us. Knowing ourselves, our feelings, and our eating patterns can help us identify the best strategies—the ones that will work best for us—to overcome our emotional eating habits.

Text-Dependent Questions:

1. List nine emotions that are most connected to emotional eating.
2. How does fear change our bodies?
3. What are three patterns of emotional eating?

Identifying our emotions, understanding their influence on our desire to eat, and recognizing our individual emotional eating habits can give us a place to begin better management of our diet and emotions. The relationship between our bodies, minds, emotions, and eating habits is a bit more complicated, however, than we've discussed so far. The next chapter takes a more in-depth look at some of the underlying reasons behind our eating habits.

Words to Understand

dehydrated: Experienced a loss of body fluids.
traditionalists: People who adhere to the customs
and practices of a certain group and resist change.
airbrushing: Spray painting to remove a perceived
imperfection.
regimens: Recommended programs designed to improve health
or fitness or to stabilize an existing condition.
legitimate: Justifiable, real.

Chapter 3

Facing Facts: Why We Eat the Way We Do

- We Eat Because We Physically Need To

- We Eat Because Our Bodies Crave Certain Things

- We Eat Because We Want To

- We Eat Because We've Been Taught to Eat This Way

- We Eat (or Don't Eat) to Satisfy a Nonphysical Longing

August 2003
Dear Diary,

I've been meeting with Dr. B. once a week for the last several weeks now. It's really helping, and I really like her. I didn't think I would at first, but she's cool.

I thought keeping a journal of what I eat and how I feel would be a waste of time, but it really hasn't been. I'm beginning to see how certain emotions trigger my binges. We've also spent a lot of time talking about how I view myself and my body and why I think about my body the way I do. I didn't realize how much I bought into the picture of "beautiful" that magazines and TV shows and movies portray. (I learned that less than one percent of American women actually look like the girls they show us in the media.) I also didn't realize how much my family's expectations and pressure from my friends influenced how I think.

For the first time I'm beginning to understand myself and why I eat the way I do. Not completely, but more than I did before. That doesn't mean I don't blow it now and then. Just yesterday I had a big fight with Dad about my curfew, and the first thing I did after our blowup was eat a whole box of Milk Duds I had hidden in my room. The weird thing was that I knew what I was doing while I was doing it. I mean, like, I knew that I was eating because I was mad, not because I was hungry. I wanted to punish somebody (Dad? Me? Mom?—I don't know) and I wanted to vent. Stuffing my face with Milk Duds was the only thing I could think of to do. It sounds so stupid, I know, but it made some kind of weird sense at the time. It didn't help, though. I just felt worse afterward.

I still haven't figured out how to handle things differently, but I think Dr. B. can help with that. I'm sure she'll want to talk about my "Milk Dud Incident" (MDI) this week when I see her. I was good, though. I recorded the whole MDI thing in my food and emotions journal. Maybe she can make some sense of it.

Well, I've got to go now. I promised Mom I'd take the dogs for a walk this morning before it got too hot. I've been doing that almost every day. It feels good. We walk for about two miles. It doesn't really feel like exercise (it seems too easy), but I have to admit that I feel better when I get back. The dogs are less rambunctious, too.

Yours forever,
Morgan

Morgan is beginning to see that anger triggers her binge eating. The food and emotions journal she's been keeping at her counselor's request shows a clear pattern of emotional eating Morgan never noticed before. Though identifying her emotions and seeing how they influence her eating decisions will help Morgan learn to handle her feelings better, these realizations don't fully explain why Morgan eats the way she does.

We stated earlier that we eat the way we do for many reasons. All the reasons can be summed up in five ways:

1. We eat because we physically need to.
2. We eat because our bodies crave certain things.
3. We eat because we want to.
4. We eat because we've been taught to eat this way.
5. We eat (or don't eat) to satisfy a nonphysical longing.

Whenever we put food in our mouths, it's for one of these five reasons. Whenever we start a new diet, it's for one of these five reasons. Whenever we start a weight-loss plan, it's for one of these five reasons. Whenever we binge, it's for one of these five reasons. When we understand the "why" of our eating habits, we'll be better equipped to control the "what kind" and "how much" aspects of the food we eat.

We Eat Because We Physically Need To

Olympic gold medalist Michael Phelps eats 12,000 Calories per day in the months of training leading up to a competition. According to an article in *Time* magazine (December 2012), he increases his carbohydrate intake to a pound of pasta and an entire pizza at every meal, and reduces his protein and fat intake during this intensive training time. Michael Phelps eats this way because his body *needs* thousands of Calories per day to maintain its ability to perform under the demands of his training regimen.

A Calorie is simply a way of measuring energy. Our bodies burn energy to function. We burn Calories just sleeping and breathing. We burn energy walking. We burn energy talking. We burn energy when we work or do laundry or cut the grass.

The amount of energy we use just to stay alive is called our *basal metabolic rate* (BMR). The BMR assumes someone is resting, and only resting, twenty-four hours per day. Any activity at all—walking, sitting up, doing dishes, reading, exercising—requires additional energy. In order to stay healthy, we need to eat at least enough Calories to cover our BMR needs. Though calculating your exact BMR is somewhat complicated, an average person of average height and weight who is moderately active would require roughly 1,500 to 1,700 Calories per day to meet his BMR needs.

Certain foods contain certain amounts of energy. If our bodies use about the same amount of energy as we consume in the food we eat, our weight stays the same. If we consistently eat more Calories than our bodies require in a day, we will gain weight. If we consume fewer Calories than our bodies need to function, our bodies will use energy from excess body fat, and we will lose weight. (Our bodies have to get energy somewhere.) So when someone like Michael Phelps is burning

Make Connections: Calculating Your BMR

Scientists use a formula called the Harris-Benedict equation to calculate basal metabolic rate (BMR) in Calories. Here's how it works:

The Harris-Benedict Equation for Males:
66 + (13.7 x your weight in kg) + (5 x your height in cm) – (6.8 x age in years) = BMR

The Harris-Benedict Equation for Females:
655 + (9.6 x your weight in kg) + (1.7 x your height in cm) – (4.7 x your age in years) = BMR

To determine your weight in kg divide your weight in pounds by 2.2.
To determine your height in cm multiply your height in inches by 2.54.

For example: Scott weighs 150 lbs, stands 5' 6", and is 21 years old. First determine Scott's weight in kg: 150 lbs ÷ 2.2 lb/kg = 68 kg. Next determine Scott's height in cm: 5' 6" = 66 inches x 2.54 cm = 168 cm. Then plug these numbers into the Harris-Benedict Equation for Males:

66 + (13.7 x 68) + (5 x 168) - (6.8 x 21) = BMR
66 + 932 + 840 - 143 = 1695 kcals per day (BMR)

Scott's BMR is 1,695 kilocalories (or what we call Calories) per day. That means he must consume a minimum of 1,700 Calories daily to perform life functions (like breathing and maintaining organ function), maintain his weight, and stay healthy. This does not include his energy needs if he chooses to exercise or be active during the day.

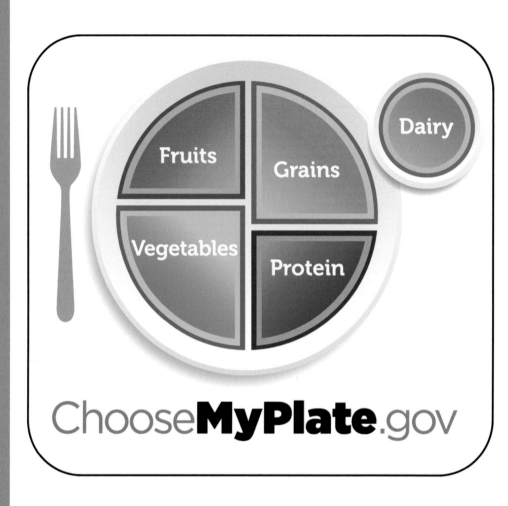

ChooseMyPlate.gov

thousands of Calories a day in physical training, he needs to consume equivalent amounts of energy to stay fit.

The U.S. Department of Agriculture (USDA) and the U.S. Department of Health and Human Services (HHS) recommends that in order to stay healthy, teenage boys and active men should consume 2,800 Calories per day. Teen girls and active women should consume 2,200 Calories per day.

When Michael Phelps eats 12,000 Calories per day, it's because he is in training and expends that many Calories daily. During his off-season, the times when he is not preparing for a race, he limits his caloric intake.

When it comes to energy, a Calorie is a Calorie is a Calorie. A Calorie from a candy bar is no different than a Calorie from a peach or nectarine. Not all sources of energy, however, provide the same benefits. Some energy sources provide nutrients and vitamins our bodies need, while others contain only "empty Calories": Calories that contain only energy but not vitamins or nutrients.

We all know that human bones and teeth require calcium to stay strong. Food products like milk and yogurt provide not only energy in the form of Calories, but calcium as well. Our bodies need vitamins A and C to maintain

Calorie with a capital "C" stands for kilocalorie. It's the amount of energy needed to heat one kilogram of water (approximately 1 liter or 4.25 cups) one degree Celsius. A small calorie, or calorie with a lowercase "c," is the amount of energy needed to heat one gram of water (approximately 1 milliliter or 20 drops from an eyedropper) one degree Celsius. There are one thousand small calories in one food Calorie.

healthy eyesight and strong defenses against disease. Fruits and vegetables provide energy in Calorie form plus vitamins A and C. Our bodies need certain vitamins, especially B vitamins, to produce red blood cells to carry oxygen to all parts of our bodies. Broccoli, spinach, whole-grain breads, fish, and other meats provide B vitamins in addition to basic energy Calories.

Potato chips, on the other hand, may give us lots of energy units (Calories) and fat, but little nutrients or vitamins. Potato chips would be an "empty Calorie" food. Chocolate, candy, cookies, cupcakes, most junk foods, soda—they all provide lots of Calories, but offer almost no nutritional benefit.

Our bodies need energy. Period. And we eat because we need to stay alive. But what we eat and how much we eat can greatly impact how we feel and how fit we become.

Eating out of necessity isn't the only reason we eat.

We Eat Because Our Bodies Crave Certain Things

As we've seen, our bodies don't just need energy, they need nutrients and vitamins in addition to basic Calories. When our bodies don't get the nutrients we need, we crave certain foods. If our bodies are low on sodium, which keeps our overall metabolisms balanced, we might crave salty foods. If we're **dehydrated**, we will feel thirsty. If we lack protein, we may crave chicken or burgers or other meats.

The source of our cravings has been the subject of debate among researchers and medical professionals. Some insist that cravings always come from an unsatisfied nutritional need. Others are convinced that cravings come less from physical needs and more from emotional needs. Still others suggest that both are true: we feel cravings sometimes because it's what our

Physically Addictive Foods
Sometimes we crave food because our bodies have become dependent on them. Some addictive foods include:

- *sugar*
- *white flour*
- *caffeine*
- *wheat*
- *refined carbohydrates (pasta, for example)*
- *alcohol*
- *certain food additives in highly processed foods*

bodies need and sometimes because of an underlying emotional or psychological need. Anyway, there's no way we can divide our bodies and our emotions into two separate pieces. Our emotional and physical well-being are interwoven.

Another cause, often overlooked, may be underlying diseases or physical conditions. One strange medical condition, which can be dangerous, is known as pica. Pica is marked by strong cravings for nonfood items: dirt, clay, paint, plaster, rust, coffee grounds, and other things we don't normally think of as food. Doctors suggest that the reason behind pica is a nutritional deficiency in the mineral found in the substances craved. If a person has too little iron in her diet, for example, she might crave iron-rich nonfoods. This was

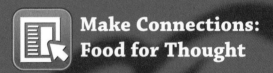

Make Connections: Food for Thought

Imagine you're sitting at a restaurant with your friends, trying to decide whether to order dessert. How would your decisions be different now from what they would be if you were alone or with strangers? A new research study suggests that if your friends eat less food, you're also likely to eat less—and even continue eating less for a while when you're alone again. The researchers found that students ate fewer cookies when their friends ate no cookies compared to when their friends ate a couple cookies. Even when the friends went their separate ways, they continued to eat fewer cookies alone if they had just watched their friends not eating the cookies.

proven to be especially true of pregnant women with iron deficiencies. Information supplied by Anorexia Nervosa and Related Eating Disorders, Inc. (ANRED), states that as many as 68 percent of pregnant women experience pica some time during their pregnancies because of nutritional deficiencies, especially those in lower socioeconomic groups.

If a doctor rules out underlying medical conditions as the root cause of certain cravings, those cravings may be rooted in an imbalanced diet or in psychological needs. In any case, cravings will drive us to eat.

Sometimes, however, we eat simply because we like to.

We Eat Because We Want To

Okay, let's admit it. Eating is fun. It feels good. It gives us pleasure. On a chilly autumn afternoon there's nothing like the taste of warm, fresh-from-the-oven, home-baked bread smothered in butter or jam. We enjoy the flavor of hot fudge sundaes melting in our mouths on hot summer days, and salty boardwalk fries when we're at the seashore or walking the grounds of a local 4-H fair can seem like pure bliss. Some foods just taste good to us, and we all like to experience pleasure. We eat because we want to.

What are your favorite foods? What do you enjoy eating most? Chances are, if these foods are set before you, you'll eat them just because it feels good to do so, whether or not you're hungry. These foods are what we prefer. But where do our preferences come from? Sometimes our preferences for certain foods develop from our family traditions or culture.

We Eat Because We've Been Taught to Eat This Way

In Morgan's first diary entry, she mentioned that on the day of her new beginning she'd eaten a cup of yogurt, fresh strawberries, and a muffin for breakfast. Why didn't she have baguette (a French bread) spread with Nutella® (a chocolate/hazelnut spread) and hot dark chocolate like many adolescents in France do? Why didn't she have muesli (a mixture of raw oats, grains, nuts, and dried fruits) served with whole milk as many teens in Switzerland have to start their days? Why didn't she prepare *uji* (a cornmeal gruel) and dried strips of beef, which is common in East and West

Africa? How about tortillas, pan dulce (sweet breads), and fried plantains (banana-like fruit), which are common in South America?

Morgan ate what she ate for breakfast because they were foods she'd learned to eat from her parents and her culture. Morgan doesn't live in France, Switzerland, East or West Africa, or South America, so she doesn't eat foods common to those regions of the world. She eats foods common to her own land. We do the same.

We also pick up eating habits from those around us. When we were young, if our parents annually served us kidney stew over waffles for breakfast on Christmas Day or Boxing Day (as is an English custom), we would probably learn to like kidney stew for future holiday breakfasts. The same kidney stew that English **traditionalists** love might be detestable to someone else who wasn't raised in that tradition.

If our parents regularly served us cereal with milk and orange juice for breakfast, we'd naturally gravitate toward similar eating patterns as we grew older. Some families never eat cereal; they eat bacon and eggs. Still others don't do breakfast at all; they just gulp a cup of coffee and run out the door. Author Dorothy Law Nolte wrote a poem entitled "Children Learn What They Live." The poem, which has become widely known and circulated, deals with attitudes and actions, but the title of her classic offers insight into how we develop our eating habits as well. We eat the way we've learned to eat. We've learned to eat according to how we've lived.

These habits can be good or bad. If we watch a parent who's under stress retreat to the living room sofa to watch TV and gorge on chips and candy, we will be inclined to handle stress the same way. On the other hand, if our parents, when under stress, exercise or work in their gardens, we might be more likely to exercise or pursue hobbies as a means to handling our own tension. We learn what we live. We do what we see.

What we live and see doesn't just happen in our families. We're influenced by our culture, too.

We Eat (or Don't Eat) to Satisfy a Nonphysical Longing

The media (newspapers, magazines, movies, TV) exists for three purposes: to inform, to entertain, and to get us to buy things. There is nothing wrong with any of these practices in and of themselves. But it's important to realize how much media influences the way we think and feel about ourselves.

When was the last time you saw someone with a bad case of acne playing a lead role in a movie? When have you seen an overweight girl standing next to a sleek Porsche in an automobile ad? How often are less-than-attractive people used as news broadcasters? They aren't. Whenever we open magazines or go to the movies or watch the evening news, we're bombarded with images of pretty, perfectly proportioned people. Beautiful blemish-free faces set atop muscle-ripped, highly-toned bodies promise us happiness and fulfillment if only we'll buy the products they sell. We, too, can look like them, they promise, if we'll only use their face cream. This hard-sell tactic includes food, too: If we eat the breakfast athlete endorsers eat, we can become all-star athletes like them, regardless of our ability or fitness levels.

It's all lies! Yet, we believe them. At some level of our consciousness, we truly think that in order to be happy or successful or worthwhile or attractive we have to look like the actors in advertisements. So we eat what they recommend or starve ourselves so we can become the images we see.

We've been deceived. Advertisers set an impossible standard. Magazines use trick photography and a technique called **airbrushing** to hide skin imperfections in their cover girls. News anchors wear heavy makeup and use studio-provided wardrobes and hairstyles to make them look their best. Some fashion models literally starve themselves to maintain their impossibly-thin figures, and they spend hours per day working on their physical

Research Project

Do some math! Using the formulas on page 47, determine what your BMR is. Explain what this means. Next, keep a journal of all your activities during a day, as well as everything you eat. Don't leave anything out, no matter how small! Go online to find one of the many calories counters on the Internet and use it to figure out how many calories you are using up through exercise. Add this to your BMR. Next, figure out how many calories you are taking in with the food you eat. Compare these two numbers. Do they balance out? If you wanted to lose weight, what would you need to do? How about if you wanted to gain weight?

fitness. Average people cannot maintain these **regimens** or use these tricks to reinvent themselves. The sad thing about it is that what we see in the media doesn't reflect what is normal, even by medical standards. Yet we pressure ourselves to meet these standards even if they can't be achieved.

Our inner longings drive us to eat or diet or use certain foods in certain combinations in the hope that our inner longings will be fulfilled, and when our new eating habits don't deliver and fail to satisfy us (as they most certainly will fail), we become discouraged and frustrated and feel like failures. Then we use food to punish ourselves.

This pattern of using food to satisfy inner longings (for beauty, fulfillment, happiness, self-punishment, and so on) and then to punish ourselves becomes a vicious, uncontrollable cycle that can trap us until we learn to put

**Make Connections:
What We See is Deceiving**

The following information, compiled from several sources including ANRED, modeling advice columns, and online secondary sources provides an interesting look at the difference between the images of women we see in advertising, stores, and toys, and what the "average" woman is.

	Barbie® doll	Store mannequin	Average fashion model	Average American woman
Height	6' 0"	6' 0"	5' 9" to 6' 0"	5' 4"
Weight	101 lbs	n/a	110 to 130 lbs.	166 lbs.
Dress size	4	6	2-4	14

One estimate stated that the chances of a girl developing a body with the same proportions as a Barbie® doll are less than one in a billion.

Less than one percent of the population fits the media-portrayed image of beauty, yet media is powerful. It creates in us a longing to be like the people we see on TV. Their lives seem so glamorous and perfect. We want to, and sometimes feel like we should, be like them.

So we eat or starve ourselves to fit their standard of beauty. Beautiful people on TV are successful and loved. We want to be successful, too. We want to be loved, so we use food to make that happen, just the way we see it on TV. "If only I could look like them," we think, "then I'll be happy."

food in its proper place. Food was never meant to be our source of comfort, fulfillment, or success. It is, after all, only food, not magic.

Whatever our reasons for eating—physical need, physical craving, sheer pleasure, habit or custom, or to fill an inner longing—it's important to recognize that food does have a **legitimate** purpose and that we can learn to use food in the right ways. In the next chapters, we'll learn how to recognize the difference between emotional and physical hunger, we'll look further at the mind-body connection, and we'll begin to develop healthy strategies for managing our eating habits and emotions.

**Make Connections:
Why We Diet**

Dorie McCubbrey, M.S.Ed., Ph.D., in her book *How Much Does Your Soul Weigh?* identifies several reasons people become weight conscious and begin dieting. Some reasons are healthy; some are not. You decide.

1. To fit in.
2. To get attention.
3. To be liked.
4. To cope with problems.
5. To compete with others.
6. To be in control.
7. To maintain a healthy weight.
8. To stay healthy.
9. To be the best you can be.
10. To be secure.
11. To escape.
12. To improve athletic performance.
13. To achieve an ideal standard.
14. To be successful.
15. To develop willpower.
16. To have your cake and eat it, too.
17. To be good enough.
18. To be perfect.
19. To be happy.

Words to Understand

interdependence: A state in which two or more
    things are reliant upon each other.
optimistic: Having a positive attitude.

Chapter 4

Heeding Your Hunger: The Mind-Body Connection

- The Relationship Between Mind and Emotions

- Hunger: Is It Physical or Emotional?

September 10, 2003

Dear Diary,

I'm back in school now. I liked it better last year when only ninth-graders were in that building; I didn't have to worry about older kids picking on me. But this year I started tenth grade. That means I had to move up to the high school where sophomores, juniors, and seniors all take classes together. I'm just a measly sophomore; the upperclassmen seem so much older and so much more together. And most of them seem fit and attractive. I feel dumpy and ugly when I'm around them, particularly in French class where there are more upperclassmen than there are kids my age. I guess that's what I get for taking accelerated languages.

The rest of the summer went well with Dr. B. I thought I was making some real progress identifying my feelings, dealing with my emotions in healthier ways, accepting myself and my body type more. I kept up with walking the dogs and started jogging some. I even went four whole weeks without binging! But now it's worse again. I feel like I'm back where I started.

I was sitting at the lunch table after school today talking with some kids about trying out for the track team, and some jock senior who overhead our conversation said in mock surprise, "You? A runner? Not with those thighs!" He doesn't even know me. What a jerk! But I was so embarrassed and ashamed. All the old names I've heard over the years came rushing back just as if I'd heard them fresh again today: blubber butt, thunder thighs, chunky monkey, moon face, forkin' Morgan, fatty Mattie. All I could think was I'm fat, I'm fat, I'm fat.

I was just beginning to get a handle on the fact that I'm not fat, really, not according to Dr. B. I just have a different body type than some. It's not better or worse, just different. But as soon as those words came flying out of his mouth I felt fat again—obscenely and unattractively fat. It didn't matter what my friends told me or what I'd learned from Dr. B. or how fit I was or what I saw in the mirror. My mind told me I was fat, so I felt fat.

What did I do? Instead of using all the techniques I've learned this summer from Dr. B., I came home and ate four peanut butter and jelly sandwiches. I don't even like peanut butter and jelly sandwiches!

Why do guys have to be so mean?

Yours forever,
Morgan

The mind is a funny thing. It can make us see things that aren't really there, like what we experience when we view an optical illusion. It can make us believe in things that aren't real, just like when we've been startled in a movie theater—whatever on the screen made us jump wasn't real, yet we reacted like it was. The mind can also make us feel very real emotions even when what we're thinking isn't true.

Can you remember a time when you thought someone was going to be angry with you about something you did, but when she found out, she wasn't angry at all? How did you feel while you waited for her to find out (nervous, anxious, afraid)? You felt those things even though what you believed about her response didn't actually happen. Your emotions were very real, even though what you thought and expected wasn't true.

Human beings aren't just physical beings. We're emotional, spiritual, and mental beings, too. What we think affects our bodies. What we believe affects how we feel and think. The conditions of our physical bodies affect how we think, feel, and act. Have you ever been really grumpy when you're tired? That's an illustration of how your physical condition affects your emotions. All people come wired with a body-mind-emotions connection.

Scientists and researchers have documented the influence of these connections several ways. In 2012, the *Journal of Religion and Health* reported the results of a study on the recovery rates of patients who were recovering from cardiac surgeries. The study stated, in part, that patients with deeper levels of religious belief were less depressed had shorter hospital stays than those who didn't hold to any faith. In this study, spirituality influenced the healing of the mind and body.

Researchers for the *Journal of the American Heart Association* reviewed several controlled studies and concluded that people with depression are more likely to develop heart disease. This connection between depression and heart disease further indicates the mysterious **interdependence** of mind and body.

Physical well-being can impact our minds and emotions. Researchers have long documented how physical exercise affects our physical health. We've all been told since we were young children that exercise is good for us for this very reason. The same researchers have also documented exercise's positive influence on how we think and feel.

Exercise causes the brain to increase the amount of certain chemicals it produces. One of these chemicals is called serotonin. Serotonin helps the nerve cells in the brain communicate with each other. Higher levels of serotonin result in better communication between nerve cells, which results in increased feelings of alertness, greater energy, and increased ability to concentrate. That's why we feel more clear-headed and **optimistic** after we exercise. Lower levels of serotonin can result in difficulties with concentration, memory troubles, fogginess in our thinking, depression, and lack of

**Make Connections:
Chronic Stress and the Need to Eat**

When our bodies undergo a sudden stress (say we're almost in a car accident), our brains tell our bodies to release a hormone called cortisol. Cortisol carries a message to the body telling it to turn on its emergency system: to become more alert, to increase blood flow to the muscles, to make energy more available for muscle use, and other life-saving responses. After a time, the cortisol gets back to the brain and tells it when the emergency is over, and emergency mode shuts down. In chronic stress, according to a team of researchers from the University of California, San Francisco campus, cortisol never delivers the "turn off" message. Part of our bodies' responses to long-term stress is to look for high-energy foods (usually high in sugar and fat) to maintain our emergency mode. We crave chocolate and donuts because they supply the short-term energy our bodies need. We also crave fat, because fat deposits in the body can send the same "shut-off" signal to the brain that cortisol sends. When cortisol stops sending the shut-off message during times of ongoing stress, eating fats gives our bodies what they need to return to a normal state.

Make Connections: The Mental and Emotional Benefits of Exercise

Most people are familiar with the physical benefits of exercise (better overall health, increased strength and stamina, stronger bones, lower blood pressure, needed weight loss, better weight management, increased fitness), but did you know that exercise can also do these things?

- reduce fear and anxiety
- alleviate sadness and depression
- reduce pain
- improve alertness and clarity in thinking
- improve memory skills
- elevate mood
- increase sexual drive
- help you to sleep better
- help you to feel more confident
- improve your self-esteem
- make you feel more energetic

(Source: U.S. Centers for Disease Control and Prevention)

energy. That's why exercise is universally recommended for people who are depressed. Exercise causes the brain to produce more of its needed serotonin, and the result is increased feelings of well-being, clearer thinking, more energy, and less depression. The more we exercise, the more serotonin is produced, and the better we feel.

We don't have to exercise strenuously to see benefits of exercise. A recent study published by the American Academy of Neurology found that even leisure activities like walking with a friend can lessen depression and reduce the risk of developing Alzheimer's disease, an illness marked by memory loss and confusion.

The medical and scientific documentation for connections between the body, mind, and emotions is overwhelming.

The Relationship Between Mind and Emotions

Consider what happened to Morgan. She was doing well in her recovery from emotional eating. After meeting with Dr. B. and journaling about her feelings, she felt better about herself, her weight, and her fitness level. Then a guy she didn't even know criticized her physical appearance.

Did Morgan's weight change when he made his rude remark? Did she magically become fat in that moment, when just a second before she felt fit? Did anything about her body change because of his words? The answer is no, of course not. Only Morgan's *thinking* changed, and because her thinking changed, her emotions changed, too. Instead of feeling encouraged by her progress and satisfied with her body type, she felt discouraged, ugly, fat, and worthless. All because of a few cruel words and her willingness to believe them.

In this case, what Morgan believed about herself impacted how she felt and what she thought. That fueled escalating self-criticism in Morgan, which led to her ultimately punishing herself by gorging on food. Her thinking (*He's right, I'm fat*), led to certain emotions (shame, discouragement, self-hatred, dissatisfaction), which triggered certain behaviors (giving up on her healthy coping strategies, reverting to using food to handle her feelings, punishing herself by gorging). This kind of thought process can lead to a dangerous cycle of repeated failure. In diagram form it might look like this:

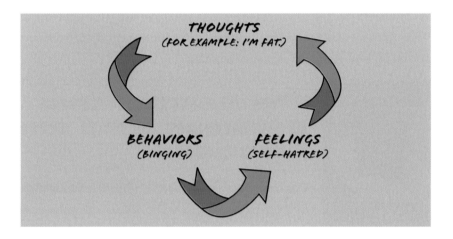

This connection exists regardless of where you begin the cycle. Maybe you'll have to start the cycle with a behavior you're not proud of (for example, cheating on a test). Then your mind tells you things fueled by what you think or believe about the behavior (*you don't deserve your friends' and family's respect; people would hate you if they knew the truth; you'll never be loved for your real self*). Then your feelings follow your spiraling thoughts (guilt, loneliness, shame, worthlessness), which can in turn drive you to further unwanted behaviors. The mind can be a powerful influence!

By now you should have some sense of how our emotions, minds, and behaviors interrelate. Where does hunger fit into the comfort food equation?

Hunger: Is It Physical or Emotional?

First, we have to determine if our hunger is truly physical hunger—a physical symptom triggering our need to eat—or if it's emotional hunger—eating for reasons other than physical need. The University of Texas Counseling and Mental Health Center cites several differences between the two:

1. Physical hunger happens gradually over time; emotional hunger comes on suddenly.
2. Physical hunger is satisfied by a variety of foods; emotional hunger usually craves one or two specific comfort foods.
3. Physical hunger is patient—it can wait; emotional hunger needs to be satisfied NOW!
4. If you're physically hungry, you'll probably stop eating when you're full; if you're emotionally hungry, you're more likely to keep eating beyond feelings of fullness.
5. After you're done eating for physical hunger, your conscience will be clear; after eating to satisfy emotional hunger, you may feel guilty or ashamed.

Physical hunger and eating to satisfy our physical hunger will have little impact on the thought/feeling/behavior connection. It's just part of our daily lives, and we give it little thought. Emotional hunger and eating to satisfy our emotions can wreak havoc with this interconnection. We tend to consume unhealthy comfort foods (foods used to create or maintain a feeling) to satisfy our emotional hunger because we seek comfort for our emotions. Emotional eating patterns, then, usually begin on the feelings part of the cycle.

Physical and Emotional Hunger Compared

PHYSICAL HUNGER	EMOTIONAL HUNGER
Comes on gradually.	Comes on suddenly.
Wants any foods.	Wants one or two select foods.
Can wait.	Feels urgent.
Goes away when full.	Continues after full.
Leaves a clear conscience.	Leaves guilt or shame.

Common Comfort Foods That Trigger Positive Feelings

ice cream
chocolate
cookies
pizza
steak
potato chips
bread

Make Connections: Different Foods for Different Moods

After studying the types of food people sought out for comfort, Dr. Brian Wansink, Director of the Food and Brand Lab at the University of Illinois, published the following research findings in *American Demographics* magazine:

Happy people preferred pizza or steak for comfort food.

Sad people preferred ice cream and cookies for comfort food.

Bored people wanted potato chips for comfort food.

Here's how it works. We feel lonely, or sad, or depressed, or ashamed, or frustrated, or frightened, or even happy. We don't know what to do with these feelings or how to handle them. Food is available: it's easy to get at, it tastes good, it doesn't argue with us, it doesn't condemn us or put us down, and it's something with which we're familiar. Like an old pair of well-worn slippers or soft fleecy pajamas, food is inviting and comfortable. So we use food to handle the feelings we don't know how to handle. Emotional eating becomes the behavior that flows out of the feeling part of the mind-feelings-behavior cycle. Our inappropriate eating leaves us unsatisfied, though, or it causes us to hate ourselves even more, both of which fuel the mind-thought part of the cycle. This in turn triggers more emotions that lead us to eat again. And the cycle continues. In diagram form, it would look like this:

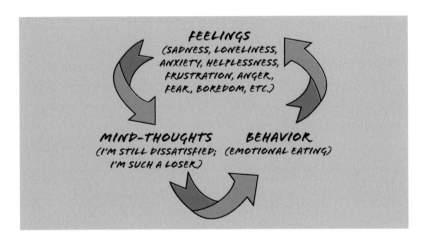

How do you break the cycle then? Can it even be broken?

Research Project

 Use an online test to find out more about your own eating habits. Here's a good place to start:

http://psychologytoday.tests.psychtests.com/take_test.php?idRegTest=1599

Do you have any areas you need to work on?

You bet! We can break the cycle of emotional eating by changing our thoughts about food and by changing the behaviors we use to deal with our emotions. We'll learn how to do each of these in the chapters that follow.

Text-Dependent Questions:

1. According to the first sidebar in this chapter, how do our bodies respond to chronic stress?
2. What are some of the emotional benefits of exercise, according to the second sidebar?
3. What are five ways to tell the difference between emotional and physical hunger?

Chapter 5

Overcoming: Putting Food, Diets, and Thinness in Their Places

- Food Is Only Food

- Be Kind to Your Body

- What's Most Important?

December 6, 2003
Dear Diary,

It's been a while since my last entry. I guess that means I must be doing better. After my peanut butter and jelly sandwich binge back in September, things have been pretty good. I haven't binged since then.

Dr. B. and I talked about what happened at school. She helped me see that there were other ways I could've handled that kid's remarks. I could've stuck up for myself by informing him of my running times and fitness levels. I could've just ignored him because he really didn't know me, and his stupid comment didn't make any important difference anyway. I could've thought carefully about what he said and evaluated his remark for what it was: an ill-informed remark by an insecure guy who doesn't know how to behave around girls. I could've thought about whether or not his comment had any truth in it at all. (It didn't—the track coach didn't care about the size of my thighs; he only cared about whether or not I could run.) If none of those worked, I could've gone for a jog and vented my anger and frustration through exercise. There were lots of other things I could've done but didn't. It was a lesson learned.

Dr. B. has been helping me see that there are really three keys to overcoming my emotional eating habits: (1) I need to remember that food is only food, then determine what I'm really longing for when I'm hungry, (2) I need to learn and use healthy ways of expressing my emotions, and (3) I need to remember to tell myself what's true (not believe all the lies the media portrays, that other people tell me, or that I tell myself).

I'm doing pretty well. I'm trying to use Dr. B.'s strategies, and they seem to be working. I made the track team, and I'm the best long-distance runner on the team. (I may be slower, but I can run for a long time.) I'm maintaining my weight and trying to eat according to Coach's suggestions and guidelines. I'm not dieting; I'm just trying to eat healthfully. I like it this way. I don't have to obsess about what I'm eating anymore. I'm trying to look at food for what it is: fuel for my body and something that occasionally gives me pleasure. Nothing more, nothing less.

Dr. B. says we can start meeting once a month now. I don't need to see her weekly anymore. She says I'm doing really well. and you know what, Diary? I'm actually starting to believe her! It feels good.

Yours forever,
Morgan

Morgan was well on her way to overcoming her problems with emotional eating. She was finally learning some important truths about food, diet, and emotions. First, she realized food is only food. It provides energy, vitamins, and nutrients to sustain health and life. It is also something that brings pleasure. As Morgan discovered, there's absolutely nothing wrong with enjoying a piece of rich German chocolate cake slathered in chocolate coconut icing if that's the kind of cake you enjoy on your birthday. It's just part of the celebration, and it is designed to be savored. But that's all it is.

Food Is Only Food

Morgan is also learning that although food is necessary to keep us healthy and fit and can give us pleasure, it can't solve our problems or take away our pain or lessen our disappointment or make our dreams come true. Food is only food; it doesn't have the power to make sense out of our lives, and it doesn't define who we are. Neither does our body size.

Carol Emery Normandi and Laurelee Roark, co-founders of Beyond Hunger, Inc., say this in their work *It's Not About Food: Change Your Mind; Change Your Life; End Your Obsession with Food and Weight*:

> We must know and feel deep in our hearts that our bodies, exactly as they are, are to be honored and respected by us. Through our own reverence for our bodies we take the first major step toward securing ourselves against violence. . . . Violence . . . means hating, criticizing, forcing starvation (dieting), ignoring our bodily cues of hunger and fullness, forcing our bodies to be something they aren't naturally, and stripping away our bodies' spiritual qualities. We can change our relationship with our bodies from one that always struggles and fights what our bodies are telling us to one that honors and empowers them. . . .When we can do this we are free to work with our bodies to manifest our dreams, whatever they may be.

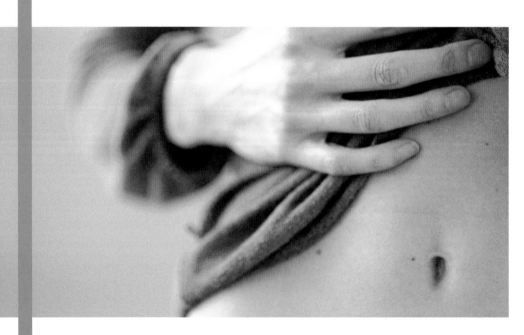

Be Kind to Your Body

Have you ever done "violence" to your own body, as the authors describe "violence" above? Do you hate or criticize your body's shape or size? Do you try to force your body to become something it's not and never can be? Do you starve yourself or ignore your body's cues telling you it's full? Do you think of your body as an object separate from your true inner self and treat it that way?

All these behaviors reveal an attitude of nonacceptance about our bodies. If I'm five-feet, four-inches tall, have large bones, a long torso, and short legs, all the dieting and exercise and emotional eating in the world isn't going to turn me into a five-feet-eleven, small-boned, long-legged beauty—and yet isn't that exactly what we try to do?

In our attempts to become something our bodies were never designed to be, we jump into the latest fad diet, we lose a few pounds, get discouraged, go off the plan, regain what we've lost, and then gain even more weight. Statistically, researchers know that most diets just don't work—not for the long haul. Consider these facts:

- According to Marketdata Enterprises, Americans spent over 60 billion dollars on diet industry (weight-loss) products in 2011.
- Current medical research maintains that fewer than 5 percent of all these dieters lose significant amounts of weight and are able to keep it off for five years.
- Ninety percent of all dieters regain at least some of the weight lost on diets.
- One-third (one out of three) regain all of the weight they lost, and then put on additional weight so that their end result is to be heavier than when they started.
- Despite these well-known statistics, a survey conducted by the Calorie Control Council (www.caloriecontrol.org) in 2010 revealed that 54 percent of American adults are currently trying to lose weight, many of them by dieting.

What's Most Important?

We are increasingly dissatisfied with our bodies and more obsessed with diets than ever, yet diets don't solve the problem for most of us. Why? More and more researchers are coming to the same conclusion Normandi and Roark come to in their book: diets just don't work—not when the cause of unwanted weight gain is emotional eating.

Make Connections: Top Ten Reasons to Give Up Dieting for Good

The Council on Size and Weight Discrimination, Inc. offers these ten reasons to resist the urge to try the latest fad diet:

1. Learning to love and accept yourself just as you are will give you self-confidence, better health, and well-being that will last a lifetime.
2. Diets can rob you of energy.
3. Diets can make you afraid of food.
4. Diets can turn into eating disorders.
5. Diets are not sexy.
6. Diets don't make you beautiful.
7. Diets don't always improve your health.
8. Diets are boring.
9. Diets are expensive.
10. Diets don't work.

The authors maintain that in order to overcome emotional eating, we must first learn to accept our bodies as they are. We must learn to value inner strengths, character, and beauty as much, if not more than, outer appearance.

Sadly, these qualities don't mean as much to us as they ought. Glenn A.

Gaesser, Ph.D., in his book *The Truth About Your Weight and Your Health*, reveals these startling statistics: Over half of the females in his studies ages eighteen to twenty-five stated they'd prefer to be run over by a truck than be fat. Two-thirds said they would choose to be mean or stupid rather than be fat. Another survey of college students found that they would prefer to marry an embezzler, a drug user, or a shoplifter than someone who is fat. Amazing, isn't it, that so many young people today feel that being thin is more important than being healthy or kind or smart or honest or law-abiding?

But is that how most Americans really feel? If it is, the country is in deep trouble. Imagine the America of tomorrow filled with skinny, "beautiful" people who also happen to be liars and criminals! No one wants a world like that, not really. Not if you take time to think about the implications. But if most Americans don't feel this way, if most still value honesty, kindness, and other virtues over thinness, then what's going on in the surveys described in Gaesser's book?

The respondents to the questions in these studies are making *value* statements about physical appearance. They are saying that physical beauty

Reason to Skip Fad Diets: Diet Ads Deceive!

The U.S. Federal Trade Commission (FTC) reviewed 300 ads for weight-loss products that ran on TV, radio, and the Internet and in newspapers, mailings, and magazines in 2004. The FTC found that 49 percent (one in two) made at least one false or unsubstantiated claim.

Research Project

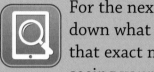 For the next week, before you eat, write down what you're feeling and thinking at that exact moment. Psychologists say that seeing your emotions on paper helps you understand what's happening inside you so that you can recognize the times when you're more likely to eat out of something other than hunger. A 2008 study from the University of Kentucky found that people choose lower-calorie foods when they are aware of their feelings. After doing this for a week, what do you think? Does writing down your feelings help you to eat in a more healthy way?

(thinness) is more important to them than health or honesty or integrity or kindness, at least for the moment. They are not thinking about the long term. That value is part of what they believe right now, and it will, as we saw in the last chapter, influence how they think and feel. Their value statements have nothing to do with food and everything to do with how these students felt about human worth and dignity.

Normandi and Roark contend that we all have value, worth, and dignity just the way we are. Most Americans, when forced to think about it, feel that way. We don't have to be thin in order to offer something to this world. We don't have to look like fashion models to love others or be loved in return. The belief that value is only found in thin people is a falsehood! How thin are your loved ones (parents, grandparents, siblings), your doctors, your teachers, your Scout leaders, your pastors, rabbis, or priests? How many of the people you love—really love—look like the models you see on TV? Most of us don't love others because of what they look like; we love them because of who they are and how they make us feel about ourselves. Why should that be any less true for how we view ourselves?

Through years of treating patients in private practice, support groups, and workshops, Normandi and Roark discovered that most unhealthy eating behaviors had less to do with food than they did with emotional and spiritual wounds that the patients in their practices carried on the inside. Their patients didn't see any lasting progress or physical changes (better fitness or needed weight loss) until they dealt with the heartaches in their souls. Food and diets couldn't solve their inner longings. Learning to love and accept themselves as they were did.

Sounds easy, doesn't it? It's not as easy as you might think. The next chapter will show us specific ways to better handle our emotions, nurture our souls, and learn to love ourselves as we are.

Chapter 6

Changing Through Choice: Healthy Ways to Feed Your Soul

To Overcome Emotional Eating . . .
 • We Need to Change Our
Thinking About Food
 • We Need to Change Our
Thinking About Ourselves
 • We Need to Recognize and
Express Our Feelings
• We Must Develop Alternate Action Steps

May 2, 2004
Dear Diary,

I can't believe it's been a year since I started writing about my struggles with emotional eating. I didn't even know that's what it was called then. What a difference a year makes!

I've grown a lot in the last twelve months and have learned a lot about myself: who I am, what I want, what my strengths are . . . but I guess the most important thing I've learned is that it's okay to be me. It's even good to be me.

When I began this journey a year ago I didn't realize how much my emotions had to do with what and how I ate. I always thought my problem was with food. Dr. B. helped me see that food was only something I was using to try to make myself feel better. Dieting was, too. Deep down inside I hated myself—I hated my body, I hated my looks, and I was scared about entering high school and hated that I was younger than so many kids in my classes. Sure, other kids teased me, and that hurt, but I blamed their teasing on me. And I hated myself even more.

Until I met with Dr. B., I didn't realize how poorly I viewed myself and how much I trash-talked to myself. I was always putting myself down, replaying all my mistakes over and over again in my head. No wonder I hated myself! I ignored anything I did right or shrugged it off as not important. I also looked at things as all-or-nothing, black-or-white. The reality, I learned, was somewhere closer to the middle.

Dr. B. showed me how to talk better to myself, to tell myself the truth. She taught me to listen to my emotions, accept them, and then do something constructive with them. She taught me to figure out what I was really hungry for (not food—that was just the surface thing, but deep down inside). And she taught me to be kinder to myself—to look for the positive, to see my potential, to accept myself as I am and to celebrate that.

That doesn't mean I don't have bad days; I do. But I'm learning to walk through them instead of running from them with food. No, things aren't perfect, and they won't be. I'm not perfect either, nor will I ever be. But I'm good enough, and I'm growing, and I'm finally glad I'm me.

Yours forever,
Morgan

Morgan has made a lot of progress, hasn't she? In the diary entry that opened this book she calls herself "stupid," "disgusting," and "fat." Just a year later she says, "I'm finally glad I'm me." What happened? Certainly all the things she described about meeting with her counselor, Dr. B., and learning to accept herself helped. The biggest change, however, occurred in Morgan's thinking.

When Morgan started her diary, here are some of the things she thought (and believed) about herself:

I'm worthless.

I'm unlovable.

I'm fat and ugly.

I have nothing to offer.

I don't do anything right.

I have no self-control.

I'll never get better.

For whatever reason, Morgan assumed these thoughts were true. They weren't. Her emotions might have told her they were; they might have *felt* true, but emotions can mislead us. Morgan's thinking was flawed, she felt helpless, and she turned to food for comfort. But the idea that food comforts us is flawed, too. Food does not have the power to comfort. It can only fill our stomachs. It can't comfort our hearts.

To Overcome Emotional Eating, We Need to Change Our Thinking About Food

Dr. B. recognized that Morgan's thinking was flawed, which is why she had Morgan keep a food and emotions journal. The counselor wanted to help Morgan see that her emotions were the root of her eating habits and that food would never heal her feelings. Morgan had to learn to recognize her emotions and use them to identify what she needed. Was she hungry for affection, affirmation, acceptance, love, approval, friendship? Once she identified her real hunger, she could learn to take practical steps to meeting that need.

Food had nothing to do with Morgan's real needs. That was the first correction that needed to take place in Morgan's thinking. The next had to do with how she viewed herself: to overcome emotional eating we need to change our thinking about ourselves.

Morgan had to learn to stop thinking flawed thoughts about herself. Was Morgan really worthless? Was she really unlovable? Did she really have nothing to offer? Of course not! Morgan had to learn to replace the false beliefs she held about herself with more accurate statements. In chart form, it might look like this:

OLD FALSE THOUGHT:

I'm worthless.

I'm unlovable.

I'm fat and ugly.

I have nothing to offer.

I don't do anything right.

I have no self-control.

I'll never get better.

NEW ACCURATE THOUGHT:

I have value just because I'm human.

People do love me. Some even like me.

I may be large framed, but I'm fit.

I can offer my love and friendship.

I can do some things well.

I can choose to control myself.

Never is a long time. A year from now
    things will be different.

Morgan couldn't just tell herself these things. She had to discover some of them along the way. Dr. B. encouraged Morgan to make a list of the things she could do or had been successful at. Morgan had to start small, but once she gave herself permission to admit there where things she really did well, her list grew quickly: she could jog; she played piano; she made it into accelerated language courses; she earned a place on the track team; she could write well; she got good grades; she could be compassionate; and she was a good listener.

Make Connections: Some Things Food Can and Cannot Do

Food can fill our stomachs.
It cannot fill our souls.
Food can nourish our bodies.
It cannot nourish our hearts and minds.
Food can make our taste buds happy.
It cannot make us happy.
Food can give momentary pleasure.
It cannot give lasting pleasure.
Food can distract us from our pain.
It cannot take away our pain.
Food can be controlled.
It does not control us.
Food serves a purpose.
It does not give us purpose.

Dr. B. also encouraged Morgan to list her "positive character traits." Morgan couldn't come up with anything she liked about herself at first, so Dr. B. had her list the positive things anyone had ever said about her (her parents, grandparents, teachers, coaches, anyone): not about what she could *do*, but about *who she was*. Once Morgan started listing some of the ways she's been complemented, she began to realize that, yes, there were some things she liked about herself after all. She just needed to be reminded.

Recognizing these things helped Morgan correct her false thinking, but she also needed to learn to handle her emotions in constructive ways.

To Overcome Emotional Eating We Need to Recognize and Express Our Feelings

Laura Spangle, RN, MA, the founder and director of WINNERS for Life (a weight-management program), suggests a five-step action plan for handling our emotions appropriately instead of turning to food. Explained in detail in her book *Life Is Hard, Food Is Easy*, her plan involves asking ourselves five questions:

1. What is going on? In other words, what's the situation?
2. What do I feel? What emotions am I experiencing as a result of this situation?
3. What do I need? What do I need to get through this or to deal with this?
4. What is in my way? What is keeping me from taking action?
5. What will I do? What actions steps can I take (not including food) to deal with this?

Morgan's situation that opened this book might have looked like this if she'd known about Spangle's plan:

1. What is going on? *Tony Penella called me a "blubber butt" in front of the whole class.*
2. What do I feel? *Angry, embarrassed, ashamed, discouraged about the lack of results I see in my running, fear that there might be some truth to what he said, and fear that I'll always be fat.*
3. What do I need? *I need to vent my anger. I need to know that I'm okay, that my body is okay just the way it is. I need to feel accepted for who I am. I need to know I'm liked. I need to like me, too. I need to feel like I'm making progress in my fitness.*
4. What is in my way? *I guess the biggest thing isn't even Tony Panella; it's what I believe about myself. I mean, my friends accept me and like me—Tony can't change that.*
5. What will I do. *I think I'll go for a run—that should help me calm down and vent a bit. Then I think I'll call one of my friends to go roller skating. Hanging around with people who like and accept me should help. And then I'll try to replace the thoughts in my head that come from people like Tony with more accurate thoughts. Oh, and maybe I'll start keeping a jogging log. Even if I don't lose weight, I'll know I'm making progress just by keeping track of my mileage and times.*

These five questions are not the only strategies available for identifying and handling emotions. Mental health professionals and researchers offer many other tips for coping: keeping a feelings journal, developing a regular exercise plan, seeking counseling, talking over our feelings with someone we trust, seeking religious counsel, practicing prayer and meditation. The point is to recognize that we feel something—and then take steps to handle that feeling in beneficial ways.

To Overcome Emotional Eating We Must Develop Alternate Action Steps

If we're honest, we'll admit that sometimes we eat when we're stressed just because we don't know what else to do. Morgan felt that way; she was so angry with Tony that she didn't know what to do with herself. Most plans designed to help us overcome emotional eating suggest coming up with a list of positive or beneficial things other than eating that we can do when our emotions want to get the best of us. Here are just some of the things experts recommend:

- exercise (walk, run, bike, hit tennis balls, swim) for ten minutes
- practice a musical instrument
- write in a journal
- listen to soothing music
- call a friend
- do something with a friend (go to the movies or the mall or for a hike together)
- work on a hobby
- write a note to someone you care about
- do volunteer work
- befriend someone who is lonely
- be a friend
- do something nice for someone
- pray for someone (maybe even for the person who's making you angry)
- walk outdoors (get out into nature)
- get a massage or a manicure

Research Project

Find out more about emotional eating. Go online and do a search using the words "emotional eating research." Read at least one study and list the facts you learn from it. Which ones are the same or similar to the information in this book? Did you learn anything new? Did any of the research disagree with anything in this book?

• read

• write poetry

• draw or paint or sketch what you feel

If you have a prepared list of things (other than eating) you can do when you feel stressed, it's more likely you'll actually do one of the things on your list, and it's more likely that you'll resist the temptation to eat. Be sure to post your list in a place where you will see it (on the fridge!).

Morgan learned to do all these things. With the help of Dr. B. she changed her thinking about food, she changed her thinking about herself, she learned to recognize and express her feelings in healthy ways, and she learned to replace emotional eating with positive action steps. Doing these things didn't make Morgan's life perfect, but they did help her overcome her emotional eating habits. And when she reverted to old, unhealthy patterns of eating, she told herself the truth: *This is only one failure; it doesn't mean I can't begin again.*

If you're an emotional eater, you're not alone. Our culture as a whole has fallen for the comfort food falsehood. But you don't have to believe the lie any longer.

Series Glossary of Key Terms

Aerobic exercise: Activities that use large muscle groups (back, chest, and legs) to increase heart rate and breathing for an extended period of time, such as bicycling, brisk walking, running, and swimming. Federal guidelines recommend that adults get 150 to 300 minutes of aerobic activity a week.

Body mass index (BMI): A measure of body weight relative to height that uses a mathematical formula to get a score to determine if a person is underweight, at a normal weight, overweight, or obese. For adults, a BMI of 18.5 to 24.9 is considered healthy; a person with a BMI of 25 to 29.9 is considered overweight, and a person with a BMI of 30 or more is considered obese. BMI charts for children compare their height and weight to other children of their same sex and age.

Calorie: A unit of energy in food.

Carbohydrate: A type of food that is a major source of energy for your body. Your digestive system changes carbohydrates into blood glucose (sugar). Your body uses this sugar to make energy for cells, tissues, and organs, and stores any extra sugar in your liver and muscles for when it is needed. If there is more sugar than the body can use, it is stored as body fat.

Cholesterol: A fat-like substance that is made by your body and found naturally in animal foods such as dairy products, eggs, meat, poultry, and seafood. Foods high in cholesterol include dairy fats, egg yolks, and organ meats such as liver. Cholesterol is needed to carry out functions such as hormone and vitamin production, but too much can build up inside arteries, increasing the risk of heart disease.

Diabetes: A person with this disease has blood glucose—sugar—levels that are above normal levels. Insulin is a hormone that helps the glucose get into your cells to give them energy. Diabetes occurs when the body does not make enough insulin or does not use the insulin it makes. Over time, having too much sugar in your blood may cause serious problems. It may damage your eyes, kidneys, and nerves, and may cause heart disease and stroke. Regular physical activity, weight control, and healthy eating helps to control or prevent diabetes.

Diet: What a person eats and drinks. It may also be a type of eating plan.

Fat: A major source of energy in the diet that also helps the body absorb fat-soluble vitamins, such as vitamins A, D, E, and K.

High blood pressure: Blood pressure refers to the way blood presses against the blood vessels as it flows through them. With high blood pressure, the heart works harder, and the chances of a stroke, heart attack, and kidney problems are greater.

Metabolism: The process that occurs in the body to turn the food you eat into energy your body can use.

Nutrition: The process of the body using food to sustain life.

Obesity: Excess body fat that is more than 20 percent of what is considered to be healthy.

Overweight: Excess body fat that is more than 10 to 20 percent of what is considered to be healthy.

Portion size: The amount of a food served or eaten in one occasion. A portion is not a standard amount (it's different from a "serving size"). The amount of food it includes may vary by person and occasion.

Protein: One of the nutrients in food that provides calories to the body. Protein is an essential nutrient that helps build many parts of the body, including blood, bone, muscle, and skin. It is found in foods like beans, dairy products, eggs, fish, meat, nuts, poultry, and tofu.

Saturated fat: This type of fat is solid at room temperature. It is found in foods like full-fat dairy products, coconut oil, lard, and ready-to-eat meats. Eating a diet high in saturated fat can raise blood cholesterol and increase the risk of heart disease.

Serving size: A standard amount of a food, such as a cup or an ounce.

Stroke: When blood flow to your brain stops, causing brain cells to begin to die.

Trans fats: A type of fat produced when liquid fats (oils) are turned into solid fats through a chemical process called hydrogenation. Eating a large amount of trans fats raises blood cholesterol and increases the risk of heart disease.

Unsaturated fat: These healthier fats are liquid at room temperature. Vegetable oils are a major source of unsaturated fat. Other foods, such as avocados, fatty fish like salmon and tuna, most nuts, and olives are good sources of unsaturated fat.

Whole grains: Grains and grain products made from the entire grain seed; usually a good source of dietary fiber.

Further Reading

Albers, Susan. *50 Ways to Soothe Yourself Without Food*. Oakland, Calif.: New Harbinger, 2010.

Beck, Meryl Hershey. *Stop Eating Your Heart Out: The 21-Day Program to Free Yourself from Emotional Eating*. Newburyport, Mass.: Conari Press, 2012.

Hanna, Melvin H. *Mood Food*. Sisters, Ore.: Deep River Books, 2013.

Koenig, Karen E. *The Food and Feelings Workbook: A Full Course Meal on Emotional Health*. Carlsbad, Calif.: Gurze Books, 2010.

Lillis, Jason, JoAnne Dahl, and Sandra M. Weinland. *The Diet Trab: Feed Your Psychological Needs and End the Weight Loss Struggle*. Oakland, Calif.: New Harbinger, 2014.

Otto, Michael. *Exercise for Mood and Anxiety*. New York: Oxford University Press, 2011.

Rath, Tom. *Eat Move Sleep: How Small Changes Lead to Big Changes*. Arlington, Va.: Missionday, 2013.

Sea Gold, Sunny. *Food: The Good's Girl's Drug: How to Stop Using Food to Control Your Feelings*. New York: Berkley, 2011.

Taitz, Jennifer. *End Emotional Eating*. Oakland, Calif.: New Harbinger, 2012.

Twelve Steps Recovery. *Cups and Scales: Weighing and Measuring Food and Emotions*. Rio Rancho, N.M.: Partners for Community, 2012.

For More Information

American Obesity Association
www.obesity.org

BlubberBusters.com
www.blubberbuster.com

Center for Science in the Public Interest
www.smartmouth.org

Diabetic Lifestyle
www.diabetic-lifestyle.com

Internationals Food Information Council (IFIC) Foundation's site for kids
www.kidnetic.com

KidsHealth
kidshealth.org

Mayo Clinic
www.mayoclinic.com

President's Council on Physical Fitness and Sports
www.fitness.gov

Something Fishy: Web site on Eating Disorders
www.something-fishy.org

TeensHealth
kidshealth.org/teen

Weight Control Information Network (from NIDDK)
win.niddk.nih.gov

Publisher's note:
The websites listed on this page were active at the time of publication. The publisher is not responsible for websites that have changed their addresses or discontinued operation since the date of publication. The publisher will review the websites and update the list upon each reprint.

Index

About the Author & the Consultant

Joan Esherick is a full-time author, freelance writer, and professional speaker who lives with her family outside of Philadelphia, Pennsylvania; she is also someone who knows firsthand what it is to struggle with weight, fitness, and emotional eating. She is the author of sixteen books, including multiple Mason Crest books for teenagers and her most popular book, *Our Mighty Fortress: Finding Refuge in God* (Moody Press, 2002). Joan has also contributed dozens of articles to national print periodicals. For more information about her you can visit her Web site at www.joanesherick.com.

Dr. Victor F. Garcia is the co-director of the Comprehensive Weight Management Center at Cincinnati Children's Hospital Medical Center. He is a board member of Discover Health of Greater Cincinnati, a fellow of the American College of Surgeons, and a two-time winner of the Martin Luther King Humanitarian Award.

Picture Credits